AF077404

I Am A Key

Clarifying Some Elements of My First Book

Emeritus Professor Larry Odell Johnson

Copyright © 2021 by Larry Odell Johnson

All rights reserved. No part of this publication may be reproduced, distributed, or transmitted in any form or by any means, including photocopying, recording, or other electronic or mechanical methods, without the prior written permission of the publisher, except in the case brief quotations embodied in critical reviews and other noncommercial uses permitted by copyright law.

ISBN: 978-1-63945-042-8 (Paperback)

The views expressed in this book are solely those of the author and do not necessarily reflect the views of the publisher, and the publisher hereby disclaims any responsibility for them.

Writers' Branding
1800-608-6550
www.writersbranding.com
orders@writersbranding.com

Contents

Preface vi
Introduction vii

Chapter I 1
    Subsection: The Alphabetical Key 4
Chapter II 8
    Subsection A: How the Derivation of an Anagram Works 11
    Subsection B: The Anagrams 14

Endnotes 66
Summary 68
References 71
About The Author: 72

I dedicate this book in solemn memory of Jackie and Robert.

PREFACE

If my books do nothing more than definitively answer the question as to whether or not everyday language conceals additional information, I will have done what I have set out to do.

My spirit suffers in ways from a profound and deep-seated sadness, brought on by the pitfalls life has bequeathed to me; once resulting in a serious tragedy impacting my life, posing unanticipated questions that everyday experiences have compelled me to attempt to answer, and causing the very best of my dreams to be deferred. I wish that I did *not* have to write these two books, but I have been emotionally constrained to do so. I did not wish and do not wish to be anything resembling a crusader or to be made to feel that I need to try and rescue the world from this or that. However, for far too many years of my life have circumstance and history robbed me of the ability to effectively distance myself and my emotions from the semblance of a crusader spirit, and prevented me from enjoying a healthier, freer, and more personally liberating outlook. Consequently, I will do no more in this book than discuss one of my keys and lend an interpretation to each of the anagrams from my first book. When all is said and done the effort might by chance or good fortune open some minds eyes, and thereby *help* to foreclose any future need for *anyone* to seriously stress or puzzle over the above question about ordinary language.

Although I have done little to try and market my first book, I do wish to thank its limited readership for their feedback…both as constructive criticism and compliments.

LOJ

1 January 2005

INTRODUCTION

My first book, **The Mind Factory**, was written with the intent of appealing to both journeymen sociologists and the lay reader as well. I had hoped that I had softened the sociological language enough that the book would accommodate both audiences. However, the feed back I have received from lay readers of my book suggest that I was not as successful in the above effort as I had wished to be. Yet despite some disappointment in my original effort, I believe that the content of my first book is vital information, and is an important enough addition to society's general stock of knowledge that I now undertake a renewed effort to clarify some of its elements. I offer this second book as a complement to the first one, and with the express intent of adding more clarity and purpose to my first book.

The Mind Factory is fundamentally a discussion about *written* language. It is a discussion about the nature of *written* language as a *social construct*. That is, man created our written language and, as a result, any fundamental discussion of written language would necessarily have a sociological orientation. (Sociology of course being a science that studies the why's and wherefores of all human activity and the history of that activity.) This orientation is the result of formal training which fosters our *desire* as thinkers to place the discussion of human experience within an historical and social psychological context. The average reader might think that these socio-historical elements are introduced solely to promote a petty elitist dialogue. With respect to my books this is certainly not the case. Moreover, it is also not the case with respect to most works that would be considered pure sociology. In fact, the real intellectual purpose is to actually demonstrate and assure the reader that what is being discussed is legitimate and true.

Like any other science sociology has its unique nomenclature or jargon. So the issue becomes how does one discuss matters that have a strict sociological orientation without using an excessive amount of the standard sociological jargon?! It is not an easy task; and may, as it apparently does in the case of my first book, require several layers of debriefing. As a matter of fact, I have discovered this need for additional explanation—quite literally—by trial and error.

My understanding and appreciation of language resulted from my having a natural ear for it from my youth. I believe I first discovered language in the tenor of my mother's voice, in church sermons—including my dad's sermons—and in music lyrics. Then, of course, my further growth in understanding language was a conscious experience honed through social interaction with other people and formal education. Because of the nature of our society and my African-American heritage, the formal side of my interaction with language was highly charged politically. That is, I became even more sensitized to language because of my intellectual curiosity and the realities of survival given the politics of discrimination in America. No doubt, my strong desire to learn a lot about the world I live in is a key element of my character and helped to focus my interaction with language as well. As a consequence, I granted or allowed my first book an organic or natural solidarity with real life experiences, by interjecting some of my own political, spiritual, and bible based commentary when it objectively flowed with the books intellectual content…which is a discussion about the nuances of language.

So as not to belabor the point, as mankind has evolved its creation of written language, it has infused certain meanings and devices in written language for strategic purposes. These purposes include the development and maintenance of linguistic tactics of secrecy, the storage of delicate intellectual and political content, and the maintenance of a *selected* historical record. My first book discusses these three primary aspects of *written language* (hereafter to be referred to simply as *language*), and places its main focus on the element of secrecy. That is, it is a discussion of how language by its very nature and design cloaks a hidden content…which is referred to as its *latent content*. Moreover, my first book suggests that the hidden content was a part of the design of language from its inception. The element of secrecy was a fundamental characteristic in the origin and creation of language as we know it. Its main purpose was not so much to communicate *as such* but, rather, to communicate human understandings and deeper meanings *secretly*. My first book affirms that this is true of everything from the most elementary forms of language to the most sublime, from the most informal elements of language to the most formal, and from the most ancient forms of language to the most contemporary.

These matters were historically discussed at length and in surprising detail by the great thinkers of mankind, but in a language that was beyond the comprehension of the common reader. I have laid out a sampling of that discussion in my first book, using the writings of certain key modern day theorists. As a result of those earlier more complicated discussions, I have arrived at the purpose of my present book. It is to give myself a second chance—allow myself a second effort—to put as much as I can of what earlier on may have seemed to some to be mere mumbo jumbo and gibberish in perspective. Of course, attempting to put the jargon in perspective was my actual intent in the first place.

Therefore let me cut to the chase. What I describe in **The Mind Factory** is that one day I discovered one can very quickly get to the hidden meanings in language with the aid or use of anagrams. The traditional or common method of creating an anagram utilizes only the given letters of a word or phrase, and rearranges *just those letters* to discover or invent a new word or phrase. The reader will find this technique to be static and limiting, because in *most cases* its application *will not* yield a solution. A solution would mean the creation of a *different* yet *meaningful content* as distinguished from that of the original content. The above technique is mechanical and only offers limited possibilities, because there are only so many ways to rearrange, that is, give a new permutation to a given group of letters.

A separate and less limiting technique in the creation of anagrams is to begin with a *pre-established* letter key, and then to use the information assigned or prescribed by fiat to the letters of the key to build the new words and phrases from the given words and phrases. This latter technique is the one I use in my first book. My approach is dynamic in that its application will eventually yield a solution that has a meaningful content in *every* case. The reason why my technique is unlimited in its search for a solution is because I allow that there is no such thing as a right or wrong interpretation. It is also to be understood that one is obligated even required to divorce themselves from moralizing or being petty and staunchly opinionated in this work. Consequently, one is permitted to utilize general information, their personal knowledge of things, conjecture, speculation, and circumspection to find meaningful contents within context. It permits one to *think* their way to a solution. That is, it enables the thinker to find interpretations that make common sense. And we are permitted to do this as long as our interpretation remains true to and *consistent* with the word *content* in the itemized *derivation* of the anagram. Moreover, one is to appreciate the interpretation of my style of anagrams as one would appreciate what is true in the interpretation of poems—and this is the likely reason that Emile Durkheim refers to these theoretical constructs as *epigrams* instead of anagrams—, understanding that the interpretational meanings of anagrams like poems will vary from person to person when individuals are left on their own to interpret them. Thus the use of a pre-established key provides us with an *objective* procedure for developing a *representation* of the derivation for an anagram. One is then permitted to use a *subjective* procedure to lend *interpretation* to the derivation of the anagram… without prejudice. However, because these latter types of anagrams are somewhat cryptic in their representation, readers of my first book appear not to have comfortably grasped what the individual anagrams expressed. Consequently, I will use the current text to interpret the complete sampling group of anagrams from my first book. I believe that effort will make those anagrams palatable to the common reader, and assist the common reader in developing a more general ability to interpret the meanings contained in their own derivations when using my style of anagram. Additionally, I am convinced that this effort will contribute to a much better appreciation for and a greater understanding of my first book. My first book then can be viewed as being analogous to the football in a football game. The ball carrier will not accomplish much in the game if the ball is not grasped properly, because the ball carrier would be likely to continually fumble the ball. My second book, **I Am A Key,** is primed to better assure that this metaphorical football will be grasped properly. For there is an amazing playing field of both intellectual and practical wisdom, that can be exploited by individuals who will properly grasp and master these discussions. *It is the kind of wisdom that eventually outpaces discussion, and is then simply to be known and used.*

CHAPTER I

The technique that I use to cipher hidden meanings that are embedded in ordinary language through the employment of anagrams is based on the possession and application of a pre-established *key*. The derivation of any given anagram is initially accomplished with the strict adherence to the use of the basis elements in the assigned key. As mentioned in my book, **The Mind Factory**, keys are to be *grown*. The original elements of a key are introduced based on a series or set of *presuppositions* that one has to have made about language and/or the realities of our everyday world. These presuppositions are sometimes referred to as "domain assumptions". Since the topic we wish to discuss is language, language is then considered to be the "domain" that we are making "assumptions" about. Thus the original elements of the key are the result of my having made certain assumptions about the origin of language. The real power in introducing a pre-established key is that not a single letter will ever go unused, and each letter will be assigned a particular meaning within context; whether or not it is already an element of the key or in its contextual application a new word is introduced that extends the elements of the key. When one is involved in the process of ferreting out meaning in the derivation of an anagram, it often happens that new elements are discovered and immediately added to the original key; when those elements complete a sensible meaning within context for the anagram under construction. This is the sense in which it is to be understood that a key *grows*, and it is the way in which an original key is actually extended.

The key that I am providing for my reader in this chapter is bigger than the key I introduced in chapter four of **The Mind Factory**. The current key is not a new or different key from the above mentioned one;

but, rather, a more grown up version of its original self. The elements of the key exhibited in this chapter that are written in *bold-face print* represent the *basis elements* and the complete set of elements that embodied the original key defined in the above book. All the other elements in this extended version of the key were added as I applied the basis elements in the construction or derivation of anagrams, most of which are not included in the book. I have included the developed extended version of the key here so that readers of my books will get a better appreciation for the fullness of connectivity, the consistency, and the continuity of thought and theory that envelops this discussion.

I have interpreted and included two hundred and eighty- eight anagrams in the present book. Each of these anagrams was constructed *solely* with the use of the bold-faced printed elements of the present key. I should emphasize and reiterate that this is only a single key grown from the few core elements. One should view the *key* as *a family of elements* with common ancestry whose source is founded in the elements written in bold-face print, and with their progeny being all of the other elements that are written in regular print. In fact this is precisely the kind of metaphor that is used in some of the classic literature on these topics. In this sense there is yet much potential for the key to grow more generations of elements. I can only vaguely imagine the tremendous amount of information gathering that could be accomplished with an even more fully grown key. I have already witnessed the power inherent in the utilization of this extended key as constituted. Experiencing the evolution of a key first hand is a delightfully stimulating and informative process. Like a player in the game of Scrabble, the practitioner is often literally forced into discovering new dictionary defined words while juggling letters in the construction of an anagram.

The key that follows is divided into four sections for the sake of clarity. Section I contains the 26 letters of the English alphabet, and to each letter there has been assigned an associated list of words and/or one or more equivalent other letters. In this section each of the words and letter combinations printed in bold-face originated from a set of domain assumptions or presuppositions if you will. They are the basis or core elements from which the others have subsequently been generated. Items in the other sections that are in bold-face print are elements which were added as original key entries for related reasons. Section II consists of letter combinations that have contextual meaning or have been discovered to have contextual meaning through the application of other basis elements. Section III exhibits letter combinations whose word meanings have been determined based on how they *sound*. The final section, section IV, is made up of elements that represent a simple but strict theoretical construct on my part. I defined a double letter combination on the criterion that states: if a letter occurs twice then that single letter is being overemphasized so it really *is*...it really exists. Here is how it works: One is simply to select a contextual meaning of the given letter as defined in the key and add the word "is" in combination with it. For example, the letter combination "dd" might read "dumb is", since we can associate the word "dumb" with the letter " d " ...as used in context and supplied by the representative key. Moreover, since the words of language are *commutative*, we can write the above expression either as "dumb is" or as "is dumb." That is, we can switch the order of the words as needed without lost of generality...without lost of definition. This construct is to remain fixed—rigid—as defined unless a double letter combination requires a different meaning within some context. For example, the letter combination "ii" could phonetically mean "aye aye" within context as in "aye aye, Sir", the acceptance of a naval order.

    I hope that my readers will develop the insight, interest, and courage to try their hand at using this key to construct anagrams from arbitrary expressions for themselves. It would be the only way for them to master the technique. As it turns out, one will discover it is an activity that is more cerebral and *much more fun* than solving the typical puzzle style manipulations. At the least, the reader should closely review the key that follows below before venturing into the reading of Chapter II.

The Alphabetical Key

Section I: The letters

- A. ***all***, any, her, author, you, anything, and, agency
- B. ***be***, bitch, bout, baby, bet, b = p, bad
- C. ***see, seem, "c"***, sea, c = k, c = z, c = s, car, cad
- D. ***dumb***, as in Ph.d, ***dark***, don, dan, damn, day, dime, do, don't, ***done***, did,
- E. ***he***, she, ***me***, we, east, see, it, thee, [note: " we " can also be equal to " implies ".]
- F. fine, fay, face, fake, faith, ***fast, fuck, fucked***, fucking, fast, "***f***", for, fact, first, fool, find, fight, foot, found, force, fee, fun, field, Friday, folding, friend, [note: " f " can be equivalent to " with ".]
- G. gee, ***game***, gain, get, good, girl, go, gone, " ***g*** "
- H. aitch, he, here, ***her, how***, h = c, ***him***
- I. I, ***me, eye***, intelligence
- J. ***undefined***, j = c, jam, j = g, j = s
- K. ***OK***, cunt, kill,
- L. ***yell***, hell, ***tell***, well, lost, tail, sell, l = t

M. him [he I am], hire him, ***him***, them, ***made***, man, high man, " hi " man, ***my***, Monday

N. ***in***, end, and, north, now

O. ***owe, own***, oh, on, out, only, no, know, old, other, ours, or, over

P. pee, peep, ***people***, pussy, power, peoples [pussy], property, permission, person, prediction, peace, press

Q. ***undefined***, que, cue, q = c, question

R. ***are, r = w, ours, hours, our***, r = p,

S. ***yes***, guess, best, ask, see, Saturday, Sunday, school, skin, south, say, is, ***street***,

T. ***time***, text, the, test, tease, turn, t = b, it, trait, t = d, at, after, tells, to, too, t = r, t = l, technology, teach, Tuesday, Thursday

U. you [" why owe you "], ugly, ***you***

V. ***v = f***, view

W. ***double you***, double cross you, wise, what, why, won, w = m, west, women, we, way, weigh, Wednesday

X. ***undefined***, exist, sex, exit, exact,

Y. ***why***, " ***y*** ", ***woman, women***, vagina, womb

Z. ***undefined***, z = s

Section II: Multiple letter shorthand meanings.

af = affect, air force ar = arrest
at = **after**
bro = **brother**
ch = choose, church, cheat, check dr = door, **doctor**, drive
eh = each equ = equal if = wife im = **I am** ld = lead
lex = **lexicon**
nt = not, neat, net

of = for, value, favor, off off = offer
oft = often op = option ot = out
rt = right, wit, wheat, wet sch = school
sh = shush
ski = skin, sky, ski
ss = **secrets, secret service**
st = **street, steak**, straight tee = teeth
th = **that**
ul = you all
wh = watch, witch, which, what yo = **flow**, you

Section III: Phonetics.

bt = **beat, bet**
def = **deaf**, deft, df, define
ez = **easy**
fk = fake
fl = fell
flo = **flow**
gy = **guy**
han = **hand**
li = **lie**
ma = **may**
mn = men
ms = mess
nd = **need**
nichel = **nickel**
nite = **night**
osa = **oh say** ("…can you see by the dawn's early light…" are some lyrics from our national anthem, "The Star Spangled Banner".)
ts = **test**
tz = tease
wah = **war**
waj = **wage**
yu = **you**
zaid = **said**

Section IV: Examples of double letter form.
cc = **see is**
nn = **in is**
uu = **you is**

As stated in **The Mind Factory**, I want to advise the reader that in developing a derivation, the procedure grants that the writer reserves the privilege of adding a minimal *few letters* to complete a minimal *few words* in an anagram, when it is necessary to complete a thought or meaning within context. The reader should refer back to this key whenever there is any question or concerns about the derivation of any of the anagrams that will be presented in the next chapter.

CHAPTER II

The sole purpose of this chapter is to give my readers an exhibition of how the method of interpretation works using an original set of anagrams. The anagrams that are being interpreted include all of the anagrams listed in chapter four of my book, **The Mind Factory**. These anagrams, which are now joined together with their respective interpretations, are listed in the precise order that they occur in the above book. However, there are also a very few new additional anagrams listed and appropriately inserted in the original list. I have included these few additional anagrams because I felt that they would help promote the overall clarity of exposition reflected in the body of anagrams. The new anagrams are based on a single word taken from the statement that produced the anagram immediately preceding it.

Since the original sampling of anagrams was all collected around the time of the occurrence of 9/11, there is an obvious continuity of exposition or common themes at times running through this list of anagrams. This continuity in information content is to be expected anyway when one is routinely collecting anagrams in sequence, as I informed the reader in my first book. It is as if one is looking at a motion picture about everyday life. In other words, proximate interpretations in the list frequently discuss the same or related topics. The anagrams the reader will review in this text are not in perfect sequence because they were randomly selected from a much larger list of anagrams. However, even anagrams from the list that must stand alone on their own merits have been assigned sensible interpretive meanings which are consistent with their given derivation.

All of the *randomly selected* statements, words, names and phrases which generated my list of anagrams were chosen from some form of public media. I have included celebrity names, book titles and related author names, news media and commercial advertising sound bites, movie titles and song lyrics, and expressions taken from ordinary everyday speech.

I routinely use some of the actual words that are derived in the anagram when developing my interpretations. Moreover, the reader will find, upon looking up word meanings from my interpretations of the anagrams, that I have maintained a very high standard of accuracy of definition and meaning. The effort toward more precision in word definitions and meaning is very important, because while anagram interpretations are necessarily subjective we should want to demand of ourselves that we stay as close to the objective meanings as is humanly possible. The demand for maximum accuracy makes the most sense in light of the fact that the interpretation of even the *same content* by *different people* has potential for a high level of variation.

Since on every level we are seeking the most objective representation possible, the more that can be done to reduce the amount of variation of interpretation the better. And this effort should be made despite the fact that no one has absolute control over exactly what the actual derivation of the anagram from its source expression will be. No matter, it is certain there is a full range of possible derivations of a given expression which can issue from this technique, and which can vary over repeated applications and from person to person. In many examples it will be obvious—and even different persons will be in agreement—as to just what the anagram means and what its interpretation should express. In other cases an anagram's meaning and subsequent interpretation will not be entirely obvious. These are the cases where one's *personal knowledge* will hold sway, and the interpretation will be at its subjective peak. It does not matter, however, because this subjectivity is absolutely consistent with the theory, as long as the *interpretation* remains consistent with and true to the content in the anagram's derivation. One need not demand much more of themselves in this process than is outlined above. It is to be understood that there are no absolute, final, right or wrong derivations or interpretations in this theory and its application. There are only derivations and related interpretations that are meaningful, consistent, and useful. However, I want to underscore there is a singular request that I and the theoretical underpinning of this theory would make of those who would aspire to expertise in this discipline; that is, when it comes to the issue of *intellectual honesty*, one bring their best or A-game to the effort.

Lastly, my interpretations of the anagrams that will follow will speak for themselves. Most of what is stated in the interpretations will be absolutely clear. Yet, as the writer, I do not anticipate that my readers will understand it all. It is in fact the case that the average reader will not know as much as I know about this subject, and it is virtually impossible for me to completely explain all the nuance…and I have not attempted to do so. Nuance along with a full appreciate of the intellectual content is to be mastered through personal application, and I have taken the major step in providing a key with which the reader can accomplish this. Furthermore, any *moralizing* about the relative value, appropriateness, and the offensiveness or non-offensiveness of the interpretations on the part of the reader is irrelevant. What *is* relevant is that the reader begins to *recognize* and *accept* that in each instance an actual content does exist; even when they know that their interpretation of the content would be different. Information gathering is the absolute intent and purpose for using the technique that is being employed here. Therefore, and generally speaking, it is *not* important that the student (as writer) or the reader (as student) *likes or agrees with* what they discover or read. What is important is that both the writer and the reader come to expect even anticipate they are *likely* to read much that they were *not expecting* to read. Each will be likely to experience new information and new twists on old—already known—information. It is this reality that comes with the territory.

How the Derivation of an Anagram Works

The first thing that I do when I set out to construct an anagram is choose any random statement, name, title, lyric, sound bite, etc. I already have the confidence that I will get a solution because I first believed and have come to know that a latent content exists, and I have developed a flexible pre-established key to assist me in the effort to illuminate that latent content. I then reread the expression several times, study, and concentrate on the expression for as long as it takes to come up with my first thought of a word that can be formed from some of the letters in the expression. Once the thought of the word is received, I write down the word and remove letters from the expression that I have used to form the first word. I then look to the *remaining* letters—repeating the above process—to suggest the form of another word. I repeat this process until all the letters have been used. In the case where I am left with just a single letter or just a *few* non-descript letters, I rely on my key to supply a *contextual* meaning for that residue of letters. If my existing key as constituted is of no help in the above regard, I simply use the given letter as the first letter in a new word within context that will give the derivation a sensible meaning. When a spontaneous new word is thus introduced to accommodate a meaning for a letter, that new word is assigned as a new element of the key for the given letter.

As a result, and at that very instant, the key itself is understood to have been and is said to have been extended or grown. Lastly, I arrange the derived words in an order that makes the most sense to me, and I write an interpretation of what I think the anagram's word content is stating. I will use anagram number 287—from the text that follows—as an illustration of this technique. And I will use a single "backslash" to indicate each space where at each step letters have been removed from the original expression to form the adjacent word.

287. Lord of the Rings: The Two Towers (an expression with two (2) derivations)

Format

The selected adjacent word in bold print: The remaining letters from the original expression in standard print.

Derivation # 1

world: \\\\ of the Rings: The T\o Towers
how: \\\\ of t\e Rings: The t\o T\\ers
sting: \\\\ of \\e R\\\\: The t\o T\\ers
h[her]: \\\\ of \\e R\\\\: T\e t\o T\\ers
foe: \\\\ \\ \\\ R\\\\: T\e t\o T\\ers
to: \\\\ \\ \\\ R\\\\: T\e \\\ T\\ers
sweet: \\\\ \\ \\\ R\\\\: T\\ \\\ \\\\\\ (Using one "r" as "w" from the last entry…as is permitted by our key.)
r[our]: \\\\ \\ \\\ \\\\\: T\\ \\\ \\\\\\
t[time]: \\\\ \\ \\\ \\\\\: \\\ \\\ \\\\\\ (At this step all of the letters in the original expression have been utilized.)

By rearranging the words of the derivation we get the following anagram:

[how / world / sting / h[her] / foe / to / sweet / r[our] / t[time]]

Derivation # 2

the: Lord of the Rings: \\\ Two Towers
two: Lord of the Rings: \\\ \\\ Towers
towers: Lord of the Rings: \\\ \\\ \\\\\\
hint: Lord of \\e R\\gs: \\\ \\\ \\\\\\
goes: Lord \f \\\ R\\\\: \\\ \\\ \\\\\\
world: \\\\ \f \\\ \\\\\: \\\ \\\ \\\\\\ (Using the letter "r" as the letter "w" from the previous entry.)

f[fuck]: \\\\ \\ \\\ \\\\\: \\\ \\\ \\\\\\ (All the letters in the original expression have now been utilized.)

By rearranging the words of the derivation we get the following anagram:

[world / hint / goes / f[fuck] / the / two / towers]

The reader may review my interpretation of the above two anagrams below at anagram item # 287.

The Anagrams

The format of the 288 entries below is as follows:

(a) The statement to be ciphered in bold-face print.
(b) One or more line-item derivations each enclosed in separate brackets.
(c) One or more interpretations of the associated line-item derivations.

In most cases I have provided an interpretation for each derivation associated with a single given expression. However, in other instances I have added *more than* a sufficient number of interpretations for the given set of derivations. The reader should easily be able to follow along with these minor variations.

1. Willa Ford [dil[do] / raw / fo[o]l]
 [will / a[f]ford]

   1. A woman who uses a dildo until her vagina is sore is foolish.

   2. A woman sharing a sexual intimacy with a friend…what do you think I use—a dildo—fool?!

   3. Someone will be able to afford something

2. A woman's threat [man / sa[say] / throw / eat]

   1. A woman feels threatened or irritated by a man who refuses to engage in the act of cunnilingus.

   2. A woman feels threatened by a man who refuses to eat her cooking.

3. * **Cunnilingus** [I / cunning / lus[t]]

It is an act that requires or displays both *cunning* and *lust.*

4. **Brown sugar** [s[h]rug / bar / own]

One should avoid being too critical of their own kind; that is, too critical of their own racial or ethnic group.

5. **Mount Etna** [mat[h] / no / tune]

    1. Do not create music by the numbers.

    2. Listening to math is not as enjoyable as listening to music.

6. **Human clone** [c[see] / name / hu[e] / lo[a]n]

    1. People can be discriminated against on the basis of the racial and ethnic information yielded by their names.

    2. Language—including names—was created by people of a certain hue (color).

7. **Thank you for having me y'all** [k[ok] / honey / hu[e] / talk / for / m[him] / fay / gain]

If Blacks speak for them through language nuance whites benefit.

8. **Attacks** [task / act]

Anything classified as an attack is a premeditated act.

9. **The transaction of obedience** [c[see] / bid / action / e[he] / then / want / o[own] / fee / so]

It is not unusual that the individual or agency overseeing the care and bidding on objects for sale in an auction would get a commission or pre-established fee for the service.

10. **Beer** [we / be]

Beer drinkers identify as a group.

11. Weather [w[double you] / eat / her]
[w[double (cross) you] / eat / her]

1. One views their world differently once they have first engaged in cunnilingus.

2. One loses their innocence once they are beguiled into engaging in cunnilingus.

12. Martin Lawrence [law / win / men / c[see] / e[he] / art]

Law prevails when men are taught or come to understand the ***he-art***.[1]

13. Thoughts about freedom [we / ought / be / fast / doom / hut]

Society ought to be quick to doom those who would war against it in an effort to force society back into the age of barbarism.

14. Horror [wow / how]

A horror is something that is at the same time both ***astonishing*** and ***puzzling***.

15. Terrorism [term / is / wow] [wise / m[him] / tow / r[ours]]

1. Terrorism is a term defining an action that elicits astonishment.

2. Wise men will ultimately protect society against terrorism.

16. One world order [o[own] / word / done / l[yell] / wow]

People will be astonished when they discover that the concept of "one world order" will inherently work to eliminate certain individual freedoms currently in existence…including freedom of speech and organized dissent.

17. Rooted out [toot / r[ours] / e[he] / d[dumb]]
[toot / r[ours] / e[he] / d[done]]

1. Anyone who would tell our secrets is dumb.

2. We will make things real difficult for anyone who would reveal our secrets.

18. Monistat [Tom[Uncle Tom] / stain]

   Anyone whose character is tainted as being that of the colloquial type labeled Uncle Tom.

19. The case of the tell tale talk show host [hat / theft / a / shock / let / tell / how / ease(easy) / lost]

   The exposure of this genre of cerebral secrets is considered a theft and is a shock. It allows one to tell how those believing it was easy to conceal information within language lost the argument.

20. Web of deceit [CEO / wife / debt]

   1. Any true CEO who is in financial debt to his wife is involved in a web of deceit.
   2. Any CEO who is not true to his wife is—socially and politically--involved in a web of deceit.

21. Operation noble eagle [eat / I[me] / nope / below / o[own] / angle]

   Engage in cunnilingus with me. No, because I think that you have a trick up your sleeve; and although that activity may be considered all American, there is something about doing that I do not understand. I suspect that somehow there is money to be made by betting on me and using this angle.

22 We're at war [we / eat / r[ours] / raw]

   We engage in oral sex so long that a woman's vagina can become raw.

23. Henry George [e[he] / why / Negro / G.E.[general electric]] [why / e[he] / G.E. / Negro]

   1. He—his character—is why the Negro generally elects to trick him.
   2. Why does he generally elect to trick the Negro?

24. Pontiac [p[people] / o[own] / act / I / n[in]]

1. There are people who own the activity in which I am involved.

2. There are people who understand all of the intricacies of the activity in which I am involved.

25. Put them out of business [pest / but / sin / mouth / o[own] / fuse]

The individual is a pest but that person's big mouth is more of a problem to themselves than to us

26. Whatever [few / hate / r[ours]] [wear / heft]

1. Few people hate our ways of doing things.

2. Exude confidence and power.

27. Attack on America [name / is / tactic / all / r[ours] / ok]

Creating and assigning names that have pre-established meanings—to people with specific assignments under our employ—is a tactic that our organization or cabal approves of.

28. Debra Burlingame [game / in / bed / u[you] / brawl]

1. Affectionately pillow fighting and pretending to fight or wrestle in bed is a game often played by sexual partners.

2. Some lovers view rough brawling or quarreling in bed as a form of foreplay.

29. Luetrell Osborne [e[he] / born / well / lot / sue]
 [sue / lot / e[he] / well(privileged) / born]

1. Wealthy people are often the targets of lawsuits.

2. Wealthy people are often obliged and able to involve themselves in lawsuits.

30. Maxine Waters [sweat / win / me / ax]

The statement refers to someone who apparently does not worry about the outcome of any kind of competition…for example a political election.

31. Sweet baby [we / by / beats]

1. We communicate with each other through the medium of music.

2. We buy music.

32. Osama Bin Laden [a / sin / me / *loan* / bad]
[I / *sold* / a / bane / man]
[no / bad / sin / a[all] / lame]
[so / me / ban / a / lad / in]

1. It is a *sin* for me to **loan** out bad men.

2. I *sold* a man who is evil and makes trouble.

3. What I do is no bad sin because most people are intellectually and emotionally lame.

4. So what, I ban kids in my organization.

33. Diane Winkler [Klan / win / we / die]

If the Ku Klux Klan—for example—were to win over their ways many would die.

34. The Hydrogen Atom: an introduction to Representation Theory [why / truth / action / wow / intent / generate / tension / mood / today / hope]

Why did those who knew allow 9/11 to happen? Their intent was to generate a necessary collective tension. As a consequence, the general mood today among those who know is one of hope that what could have been—the destruction of civil society—will never be.

35. Haverford College [have / our / leg / is / cool / def(deft)]

Be assured that all of our coeds are cool and smart.

36. Lights, camera, action [malice / has / traction / g]
[great / action / h[he] / claims]
[lactation / came / r[ours] / sigh]
[white / lion / act / a / scam / game]

1. Malice can be an effective tool in ones effort to influence another person to some type of action.

2. He claims it is great action.

3. A female's lactation elicited an audible sigh of pleasure.

4. The white lion act in Las Vegas is a possible scam game.

37. Raise up [a[all] / wise / up]

All people should wise [smarten] up.

38. Evgeni Plushenko [feeling / poke / h[he] / n[in] / us]

Women can feel the penile poking during coitus.

39. We right here [we / weight / her] [wire / her / get / h[he]]

1. We credit her with having a degree of influence and a level of importance.

2. Wire the woman with a hidden microphone and we will get the guy.

40. Igor Lukashio [I / law / skin / u[you] / go]
[I / go / u[you] / law / skin]

1. You need to get out of here, **mine** is the skin color of the law.

2. When **my** skin color is no longer the color of the law **your** skin color will be the color of the law.

41. Tian Liang [a / gain / lit / n[in]]
[n[in] / gain / lai / t[time]]

1. An obvious gain encouraged those involved.

2. Those involved gain the time to write lyrical poetry...music

42. Aleksandr Variamov [drama / so / flaw / fake / n[in]]

Some emotional drama occurred and that only means that there is a fake individual involved in this.

43. Irina Lobecheva [achieve / win / o[owe] / lab]

If we achieve a win we will owe and must give much of the credit to those who worked with us at our *training laboratory* for athletes.

44. Show me where you layed your brother down [there / how / her / own / read / yes / you / would / my / bro[brother]]
[yes / her / would / own / how / you / read / there / my / bro[brother]]

1. If the information reveals the ways in which their own come to read so well, then that information would help you to achieve that reading level also my brother.

2. Yes, she would be in charge and determine just what exactly it is you learn there my brother.

45. Mohammed Atta [mm[him is] / tamed / aa[all is] / hot]

We (Al Qaeda) will have tamed America when we have carried out our 911 plan, but then things will be hot because we will all be wanted men.

46. Wiretap expansion [war / a[all] / p[people] / exit / pension]

There are those who are aggressively and vigorously seeking to undermine traditional employee retirement benefits.

47. Ayub Ali Khan [a[all] / yu[you] / b[be] / a[all] / li[lie] / k[ok] / han[hand]?!]
[yu[you] / be / a[all] / k[ok] / a[all] / han[hand] / li[lie]]

1. Not all of us are who we claim to be...ok buddy.

2. We claim that we will be ok, but we all know that is a lie.

48. Preparing for war [we / p[people] / pawn / grow / fair]

For the time being we are declaring a moratorium on being fair.

49. Eric Darton [note / I / c[see] / draw] [I / draw / " c " / note]

1. For the record I see it as a draw.

2. I made a hundred dollars.

50. Gary Tuckman [many / track / u[you] / g]

There are many who follow you because of who you are my friend.

51. Richard Grasso [so / hard / was / I / c[see] / r[ours] / g]
[I / c[see] / r[ours] / was / so / hard / g]

1. It has been very difficult for me to understand just who we are my friend.

2. Now I understand—from personal experience—how hard it is for people to truly understand themselves.

52. Order [wow / e[he] / d[dumb]]
[wow / e[he] / d[done]]

1. He takes orders so he must be dumb.

2. The evil deed is done.

53. Zaid Jarrah [zaid[said] / waj[wage] / wah[war]] (phonetic)

We were told to wage war.

54. Osama Bin Laden [osa[oh say/U.S.A.] / ma[may] / b[be] / in(internally) / laden(burdened)]

The United States of America can be weakened from within… (presumably by acts of terrorism within its borders.)

55. Emergency Medical Technician [rim / agency / hit / menace / c[see] / decline]
[menace / hit / agency / c[see] / dim / recline]
[agency / c[see] / decline / menace / hit / rim]

[magician / nichel[nickel] / end / tee / c[see]]

1. The Pentagon was hit and those responsible will pay a heavy price.

2. A menace hit the Pentagon because they caught the U.S. napping.

3. The CIA reduced counterintelligence spending, so a menace got the courage to hit the Pentagon.

4. Those responsible for financing 9/11 actually ended the relax and see attitude of the USA defense agencies, and gave the USA an early warning; before the foreign terrorist networks could embed themselves too deeply into the American homeland.

56. Alexis On Fire [o[own] / fine / is / relax]
[o[on] / is / fine / relax]

1. Your girlfriend is beautiful…so relax.

2. Being truly hip to what is going on in the world is not a problem…so relax.

57. Harvey Kushner [he / y[why] / far / knew / us]

1. Foreign nations have come into their own is why many feel less indebted and beholding to the United States.

2. We are masters of the he-art is why some other nations may resent the United States.

58. Future of terrorism [wow / is / term / for / uu[you is] / " f "[fucked] / e[he] / t[time] (" it " me)]

Wow is a term—within context—meaning you are fucked, because your modern day understandings of our secrets have hurt me.

59. Sylvana Soligon [song / lion / " f "[fucked] / slay / a[all]]

Our ability to communicate secretly via the powerful medium of music has prevented the destruction of the United States.

60. Peter Gold [got / deep / r[ours] / l[yell]]

[go / deep / r[ours / tl[tell]]

1. Got deep penile penetration and the woman yelled.

2. Succeed in getting deep sexual penetration and a woman will tell other women.

61. Dr. Cheryl Arutt [Dr[doctor] / c[see] / her / " y " [vagina] / a[all] / l[yell] / r[hours] / tt[time is] / u[you]]
[Dr[doctor] / c[see] / " y " / her / a[all] / l[yell] / r[hours] / tt[time is] / u[you]]

1. A doctor evaluates a pregnant woman's vagina and declares she is fully dilated, and then the nursing staff and all others present yell the baby will certainly be delivered within an hour's time.

2. A doctor is manipulating a woman's vagina and she is yelling as the baby is being delivered.

62. Presburger Groups (from mathematical theory)
[soup / burger / grew / p[people]? / s[yes]!]

Have the additives in our food caused people to grow physically? Yes!

63. Richard Kaye [key / hard / I / wac[wack]]

Anyone who thinks this key is hard is crazy.

64. Edward Cardinal Egan [dead / "g" / n[in] / car / denial / war] [2]
[car / n[in] / "g" / dead / denial / war]

1. A body is found. It was an ordered professional hit. The organization will deny it…signed: ***War.***

2. A hit is ordered. The hit is carried out. The organization denies responsibility for it…signed: ***War.***

65. Pentbomb [p[people] / be / n[in] / tomb]

People have been entombed.

66. Joe Lhota [jot / a / hole] [jot / o[own] / heal]

1. Jot down that there is indeed a hole at Ground Zero.

2. Jot down that our nation will eventually heal from this wound.

67. Deepika Sarttalure [keep / date / as / u[you] / r[ours] / tail]

1. Be sure to keep appointments because someone is tailing (following) you and/or keeping tabs on what you do. .

2. Be sure to keep our date because you are my sexual partner.

68. Omar Wasow [wam[wham] / o[owe] / so / war]

Those who attacked us owe so that means war!

69. Alexander Degrand [lex[lexicon] / and / we / a[all] / grade / n[in] / d[dumb]]
[lex[lexicon] / and / we / a[all] / grade / n[in] / d[done]]

1. Reveal the secrets of the lexicon and we will all label one of our own dumb.

2. Reveal the secrets of the lexicon and we will say the education of one of our own has been completed.

70. * Dumb [d[do] / u[you] / m[him] / b[be]]

Do you he is! (...That is, learn these secrets for yourself as well, because he already knows them.)

71. Samuel Kassow [k[ok] / amuse / low / ass]
[k[ok] / a / low / ass / muse]

1. Alright, amuse the low ass.

2. It is ok if the low ass is a muse.

72. Trinity College Professor of Italian Studies [city / wit / n[in] / profess / roof / e[he] / it / own / leg / l[yell] / stud / is / a / alien[UFO]]

If a person is raised to know the ways and wit of the city streets and is willing to discuss those secrets openly, that person is *it*...that is, the person is to be labeled an oddball. Even his own girlfriend would declare him an alien.

73. Susan Zuccotti [out / cuss / saint]
   [s[yes] / cuss / aint / out]

   1. Some outside of the church curse the saints.

   2. Yes, using invectives is not taboo.

74. Under His Very Windows: the Vatican and the Holocaust in Italy [h[he] / do / win / dear! / y[why?] / hint: / cause / low / friend / has / talent / fist / can / hit / you]

Let him win dear. Why, because our low life friend has a talent?! He does not mind engaging in fisticuffs and will hit you.

75. Silent No More: confronting America's false image of Islam
   [silence / is / a / lame / front / o[own] / forgot / saga / mnemonics / fire / a[all] / mail]

Not being willing to discuss these things is lame and a front. It reveals that those who were responsible for memorizing the story in its historical detail—through the use of mnemonic devices—forgot everything, and they do not want that fact to be revealed. Therefore, it is best to discard most of the information coming from those oral tradition sources or mail carriers—if you will.

76. Hitler, the War and the Pope [peep / and / l[yell] / thwart / her / own / hit]
   [peep / and / l[tell] / thwart / her / own / hit]

   1. Looking ahead and making a deal with Hitler and his regime prevented the destruction of properties and artifacts belonging to the Catholic Church during WWII.

   2. The Catholic Church agreed to do so and protected war criminals at the end of WWII.

77. **Hartford, Connecticut** [hard / t[time] / for / I.D. / cut / connect]

A person is having a hard time now that their true identity has been revealed.

78. **Earring** [win / gear] [gear / win]

   1. Win designer clothing.
   2. Designer clothing is associated with people who want to be winners and with being a winner in general.

79. **Ear piercing** [I / creep / a[all] / grin]

A pierced left ear—traditionally—identified a male as a player…a worldly streetwise person and/or a womanizer.

80. **Payne Stewart** [pay / nest / e[he] / war / time]

Attempts were possibly made to extort money from Payne Stewart—or some facsimile—but it was refused…result: The person is out of time.

81. **Emeril Lagasse** [s[yes] / sage / wile / meal]
   [meal / sage / wiles]

Yes, this profoundly wise man devotes his skills to creating cunning or clever meals.

82. **John Hope Franklin** [join / open / hh[he is] / k[ok] / ran / f[fast]]

Told to either join the organization or suffer consequences the person did not join but is ok. The person saw an opening or opportunity to get away and so ran fast to safety.

83. **My life and an Era** [if / year / land / mean]
   [I / fear / land / y[why?] / mean]
   [I / fear / land / e[he] / many]
   [many / e[he] / I[eye] / land]

   1. If it takes a year to accomplish this country is mean.

2. I fear this country because its people are mean.

3. I fear this country because there are many who are in the know.

4. This country keeps an eye on many people, so it is a country that is to be feared.

84. Happily ever after [happy / lie / few / rate / " f "]
  [happy / lie / " f " / rate[benefit] / few]

1. Happy people are lying when they say many give an " f " a good rating.

2. The idea that people who receive a rating of " f " –from graduate school education—are happy people is a lie. Few people receive rewarding benefits in a natural way from such a rating.

85. Breath [we / b[be] / a[all] / th[that]]

We have ourselves together and stand above the crowd in every way.

86. Dr. Jorge Piedrahita [what / died? / rape / r[ours] / I / jog]

What attitude died? The attitude that allowed you to rape my people, and all the while I would ignore it and pretend not to have noticed.

87. Ana Robar [o[owe!] / a / bar / ran]
  [o[own] / ran / a / bar]

1. You owe. We barred the person and you let the person get away.

2. A family member once owned and/or ran a bar.

88. Law and Order [law / down / a[all] / wed]

If you are down to achieve your best you need to settle down and get married.

89. Elvis Stojko [list / of / jokes]

1. It is a list of jokes.

2. The list will off or end the jokes.

90. **Johnny Weir** [why / coin / [k]new]
    [why / new / coin]

    1. Why I recognize that the wealthy knew of the event before it actually took place.

    2. Why create a new coin?

91. **Alexei Yagudin** [exude / gain / I / lay]
    [lay / I / exude / gain]

    1. One who is ostentatious or showy in wealth is naïve.

    2. I am naïve if I am showy (bling bling) with wealth.

92. **Nail it down and we've got motive** [down / to / give / of / time../ nail(date) / ant(work) / wed]

    If you are committed to giving of your time to another find someone special to date, land a good job, and then get married.

93. **Salve Regina University** (*Save Vagina* University…my emphasis) [law / unity / see / virgin / safe]
    [see / virgin / safe / law / unity]
    [safe / virgin / unity / law / see]

    1. The law at our college is our commitment to staff and student unity, and to seeing that our virgin coeds retain their virginity during their tenure here.

    2. Seeing that our coed virgins remain safe from the temptation towards promiscuous behavior is a law that we are united over at this college.

    3. The legal system respects our safe virgin policy.

94. **Sister Therese Antone** [see / st[street] / the / wise / want / one(a virgin)]
    [st[street] / see / the / wise / want / one]

1. The street needs to understand that wise men want to marry women who are virgins.
2. The street does understand that wise men want to have virgins to wed.

95. Christina Otero [choose / wine / wit / t[time]]

We coeds choose to sip wine, use our wits, and postpone our initiation into sexual activity.

96. Mary Roosa [room / was / y[why] / a[all]]
[room / " y " / was / a[all]]

1. There was room is why we placed her there.
2. To have places for more women to stay was the sole reason for our actions.

97. Complete Dell system [c[see] / y[why] / st[street] / let / me / sell / mop[my own people]]
[sect[yes he see time] / let / me / sell... / mop[my own people] / d[dumb] / y[why]]

1. *Try to understand why the street let me sell my own people.*
2. *Yes he sees the history of my people selling themselves... even into slavery. That historic behavior survives because my people are dumb.*

98. "Hello Mrs. Lindsey" [hey / Ms. / d[dumb] / in / sell / low]

Listen to this Miss, only the dumb sell low.

99. "You're not by any chance computer shopping are you?"
[pry / can / come / hoping / you / buy / share / put / note / way / one / c[see]]

Nosey people will come hoping to see you buy shares of the business. Place a notice of the time and location of the event where it will be visible to them and for their benefit.

100. " She intrigued? " [sin / he / quit / wed]

[he / quit / wed / sin]

1. It is really a sin that he got a divorce.

2. He got a legal divorce from a bad marriage.

101. " Thanks Stephen " [hen / pest / th[that] / sank]
[hen / step / thanks]

1. The impression that his woman is a pest was not convincing.

2. He is thankful that when he asked his woman to leave she did so.

102. Phil Keoghan [hi / h[he] / n[in](created) / geo(the earth) / lap]

Hi, my name identifies me as the guy who created the " circle the globe " event.

103. Secretary [secret / a[all] / r[ours] / y[why]]
[r[ours] / a[all] / secret / y[why]]
[a[all] / r[ours] / secret / " y "]]
[a[all] / secret / " y " / r[ours]]

1. The secret is ours alone is why.

2. Why? Because everything we are involved in is a secret!

3. We all keep our women secret.

4. We consider all discreetly private women ours.

104. Wanted [ant / wed]
[wed / ant]

1. The workaholic got married.

2. Marry a workaholic.

105. Check it out [c[see] / heck / it / out]

One's having the ability to see that something is trouble before getting involved in it enables one to avoid the trouble.

106. Alphonso Capone [phone / on / c[see] / soap / a[all] / l[tell]]
[phone (phony) / soap / on / c[see] / a[all] / l[yell]]

1. People often discuss the soap operas over the telephone.

2. Addicted people often get into a panic to quit whatever they are doing to be in time to watch a phony soap opera.

107. Great [r[ours] / eat / g[game]]
We eat meat.

108. Can you stand to be great? [g[game] / r[ours] / bet / o[own] / and / you / can / eat / st[street]…[steak]…[yes time]]

Do as we do in our game where we create or allow scenarios that enable us to bet on our own people, so that you will be able to afford to party, eat well, and have a lot of free time…just like we do.

109. Anxiously waiting to be deployed [existing / deed / only / ploy / bait / o[own] / a[all] / u[you] / w[double you]]
[existing / deed / only / ploy / bait / you / a[all] / o[own] / w[double you]]

1. The existing deed is only a ploy. Think about it. You use your own as bait and in the end all you do is double cross yourselves.

2. The existing deed is only a ploy. Use yourself as bait and all will eventually see both sides of who you are.

110. Probably means about two and a half hours [aha / left / doubt / ours / saw / woman / baby / plan / oh]

Our exclamation—aha!—actually left doubt in the minds of those observing that we had already foreseen the woman's baby plans. Oh!

111. Don't say a word [don[e] / way / road / st[street]]
[st[street] / don / roadway]
[don / road / st[street] / way]
[stay / down / a[all] / r[ours] / do]

1. The street's roadway is done.

2. The street is a gangster don's roadway.

3. The don was gunned down.

4. Stay committed to working from behind the scenes because that is the way we all do things.

112. **Invectives** [stiff / see / in]
 [see / in / stiff]
 [in / see / stiff]

1. One is typically near the end of their lives by the time they are able to fully comprehend and appreciate the significance of the he-art.

2. See your own way in and you are dead.

3. Made members of the group see you as a dead person.

113. **John Michelotti** [hit / lot / him / c[see] / Joe / n[in]]

Hit the whole group of people and one will know that the government is involved.

114. **Tom Sluiter** [to / m[him] / it / slew / u[you]]

To the outside observer your mere involvement caused you to be killed.

115. **Never too far** [few / won / o[own] / fate]
 [few / [k]now / o[own] / fate]

1. Few people have won control over their own fate.

2. Few people know their own fate.

116. **Chadeen Palmer** [law / me / e[he] / had / c[see] / pen]

Kill me and my associates will no longer assist you in deciphering future events.

117. **Glacier National Park** [page / work / l[tell] / I / act / anal / in]

Academics and other white collar workers who do a lot of paper work are often said to act anal...that is, to be excessively neat and particular.

118. Western wildfires [dire / news / west / if / w[double you] / l[tell]]
[news / dire / west / I[eye] / " f " / l[tell] / w[double you]]
[if / r[ours] / die / west / news / l[yell] / w[double you]]

1. It will be dire news west coast if one of those you trained tells.

2. The news is dire west coast, one of your " f 's " is explaining our *double entendres*...the very essence of duality.

3. If one on the east coast dies west coast the news media will yell information about the opposing sides.

119. Matt Rainy [aint / my / tar] [aint / my / rat]

1. That aint my nigger.

2. That aint my snitch.

120. Building [lid / bug / in] [lid / bug[g]in]

1. Someone is eavesdropping.

2. You guys are bugging out...are going crazy.

121. Bob Blau [blab / u[you] / B.O.(bad odor)]

Go ahead and blab you are nothing but a bad odor anyway.

122. Newark [wake / r[ours] / n[in]]

Please make ours aware also.

123. Mark Seibel [seem / I[eye] / b[be] / lark]
[bar / milk / see]
[milk / be / e[me] / was]

1. It seems to me the idea that there exist entities that can actually see through our own eyes is a lark.

2. Why not discourage adult milk drinking if you truly understand the side effects of the lactose intolerance that is common to most adults.

3. As an adult, I no longer am a whole milk drinker.

124. Amy Fickling [many / lick(beat) / fig]

Many people stop eating delicious fig products because they can cause gastro-intestinal problems.

125. Dr. David Faxon [now / did / fad / fax]

New age people have made faxing a fad.

126. Heather Graham [eat / her / hag / ham / r[ours]]

If one of our buddies becomes sexually intimate with and engages in cunnilingus with her hideous female friend he is naïve and desperate.

127. Lifetrack [lift / race / k[ok]]

Doing things that are elevating to your race is ok.

128. What if [faith / w[double you]]

One needs *faith* in order to completely understand the hidden wisdom of the he-art.

129. Love of my life [foe / fly / me / foil] [fly / me / foil / foe]

1. We have succeeded in foiling a terrorist's easy access to boarding our passenger aircraft.

2. As the general public continues to use passenger aircraft as a popular mode of transportation, they foil what the terrorists sought to do on 9/11…shut down our airline industry.

130. I'm lookin' [m[him] / ill / no / ok]
  [ill / m[him] / no / ok]

1. It is not ok when someone is ill.

2. It is not ok to make someone ill.

131. Charles Payne [help / saw / c[see] / nay / e[he]]

One of our helpers witnessed us *apparently* deny entry into our inner circle to one of our *initially* chosen.

132. Former Deputy Director of State Dept. Office of Counterterrorism [o[own] / foot / error / fate / enter / dispute / come / dry / pit / suffice / from / d[dumb] / rector(school/church) / t[time]]

The way in which we publicly aired our differences over defense spending allowed fate to enter the dispute. The result is that you need to come and help clean up the mess at Ground Zero. This is the opinion of our so-called dumb educators and clergy.

133. Training Day [grid / aint / nay] [nay / grid / aint]

1. Football is not a negative activity.

2. Eliminating football as a sport is not an option.

134. Mary Schiavo [I / fay / so / charm]
[fay / so / I / charm]

1. I am a white person so charm me.

2. I am a white person and it is a characteristic of mine to charm people.

135. C. Virginia Fields [c[see] / lid / I[eye] / virgin / safe]
[c[see] / virgin / lid / I / safe]
[safe / lid / I / c[see] / virgin]
[lid / safe / I / c[see] / virgin]

1. After exploring the content of the girls mind power "*Eye*" (as defined and discussed in my book **The Mind Factory**) can verify that the girl is still a virgin.

2. If they see a virgin mind I am safe.

3. Strong young female mind and I see a virgin.

4. Her mind is a safe, so I see a virgin.

136. Wanted dead or alive [live / read / want / o[own] / add / e[he]]
   [want / dead / live / o[own] / read]
   [oral / deed / want / a / dive]
   [dan / t[time] / deal / adore / wife]

1. Just live, study, and desire and your own will comment that you are mature.

2. *If you want a dead mind to live you must make reading a part of your lifestyle.*

3. I do not want to get involved in oral sex.

4. If you want to master life be true to your promise to be faithful to and adore your wife for life.

137. Right Guard deodorant [hard / order / aint / do / t[time] / gg[" g " is] / u[you]]
   [hard / order / aint / rug / do / t[time]]

1. Our order was not that you should do jail time. You are the **one**…a special person.

2. It was not our order to give you a rug (rectal condyloma) and have you serve time in jail.

138. Victoria Toensing [wait / fiction / so / e[he] / g[game] / n[in]]
   [fiction / wait / so / e[he] / " g " / n[in]]

1. Having to wait is a fiction and a ruse, so he/she is trying to fool you.

2. Pretend to wait and then go do something else, so that he/she will know you are not a fool.

139. Robert Crandall [down / wall / be / tar / c[see]]
   [down / wall / brat / e[he] / c[see]]

1. What is being hidden is that dark skinned people do understand.

2. What is being hidden is that he is a brat.

140. Robert Butterworth [we / wow / but / the / rot / time / b[be] / r[our] / tow]

While we continue to wow him the majority of jail time falls to us as our responsibility.

141. Crusade [ruse / cad]
[cad / ruse]

1. It is a stratagem that we are always cast as behaving dishonorably… as criminals.

2. Pretending to be a bad boy is a trick.

142. Roger Porter [w[double you] / we / grew / o[own] / pot] [pow / wet / o[own] / grew] [4]

1. To get around you we grew our own pot (marijuana).

2. We shot one of theirs and as a consequence the number of our own dead and wounded increased.

143. Amada Grove [wave / a / d[dumb] / man / go]

Do not get involved with a dumb man.

144. Fond exit [fix / t[time] / done] [t[time] / fix / done]

1. The time is set.

2. Time it, fix it, and be done.

145. Aileen Sigany [glean / any / II[I is] / s[yes]]

Do you understand any of it? Yes!

146. Ceasefire [c[see] / ease(easy) / fire]
[ease(easy) / c[see] / fire]
[fire / ease(easy) / c[see]]

1. If the person is an easy *mark* fire them.

2. Easy to see then take the shot.

3. Fire anyone who thinks what we do is easy.

147. Khaled Safouri [loud / hair / safe / k[ok]]
[hair / safe / loud / k[ok]]

1. Colorful hair is safe, ok!?

2. If no one is at risk being loud is ok.

148. James Zogby [a / mess / jog / by]
[jog / by / a / mess]

Do not rubberneck.

149. Sister thy brother is seated [rather / try / o[own] / the / best / sis / side]
[sis / rather / try / o[own] / the / best / side]

Most people have a strong feeling that dating within their own racial or ethnic group is best.

150. Something in the past [past / e[he] / thing / so / them / Im[I am]]
[past / e[he] / them / so / Im[I am] / thing]

I am the opposite of whatever he was to them in the past.

151. Inferior [fine / I / wow]
[wow / I / fine]

1. I wow pretty people.

2. I look good.

152. Jack Zelmanowitz [jazz / man / cloke / wit]

There are hidden messages even in jazz music.

153. Fallin [ill / fan]

An overzealous fan is considered ill.

154. Area codes [does / we / c[see] / aa[is all]]

The question is do we understand!?

155. Caramel [law / came]

The law was enforced!

156. Obstetrics [wit / st[street] / c[see] / be / so]
[so / be / wit / st[street] / c[see]]
[so / wit / be / c[see] / st[street]]

1. The wisdom of the street is real!

2. Be someone who can relate to the street and visa versa.

3. When one understands street wit one can understand the streets.

157. Nabil Al-Marabh [nab / m[him] / a / hall / Rabbi]
[a / hall / Rabbi / nab / m[him]]

1. He caught a Rabbi involved in a wrongdoing.

2. He wants to kidnap a Rabbi

3. That teacher is a Rabbi so seize him.

158. Anjem Choudary Al-Mouajiroun [major / name / could / join / aa[all is] / uu[you is] / why]
[major / name / is / why / you / could / join / is / all]

1. Your *name* is important enough to our group that you may join us.

2. Your *name* is the sole reason why you would be allowed to join our organization.

159. Hardball [w[double you] / bad / hall]

Any educational institution that schools one in the hidden wisdom is considered an unlawful or bad school.

160. California love [I / call / own / if / a[all] / foe]
[I / call / own / if / a / foe]

I would disown my own relatives if they turned out to be my enemies.

161. Single white glove [fog / l[tell] / sin / we / hit / glee]

Some people in the Bay Area would admit their biggest sin is that they act out against individuals who exhibit what they consider to be having too much fun, and also those who exhibit too much laughter.

162. Confidencc [c[see] /e[he] / confide / n[in]]

Make sure that he becomes willing to confide in you.

163. Arabic [a / Rab[b]i / c[see]] [see / a / Rab[b]i]

1. A Rabbi understands.
2. Ask a Rabbi to explain it.

164. Pragmatism [gramma / tips]

One will get tips from this School of Philosophy on understanding grammar.

165. White Cadillac [a[all] / c[see] / we / hit / ill / cad]

Everyone can know that we hit someone who we considered to be emotionally unstable and disrespectful to women.

166. Donald Rumsfeld [Mad? / s[yes!] / d[dumb] / found / well]
[Mad? / s[yes!] / found / well / done]
[fun / road / smell / dd[is done]]

1. People are mad (angry) because they consider the person to be dumb.
2. People are mad (angry) because he has been approved for the job.
3. He can enjoy the ride now that he has defeated his opponents.

167. Operation Enduring Freedom [me / end / waiting / proof / we / done / u[you]]
[end / we / waiting / proof / done / u[you] / me]
[doom / ending / r[ours] / free / we / taping / u[you]]

1. We are no longer awaiting proof we have already decided to accept you.
2. Forget trying to destroy us, we are now freed to spend our time taping and monitoring you.

168. Zoolander [so / do / learn]

Be willing to learn.

169. Fly fishing [if / shy / fling]

If you are shy overcome your shyness by simply taking advantage of an opportunity to go hog wild.

170. The next of kin to the wayward wind [he / o[owe] / kin / text / win / war / font / way / he / is / time / done]

He owes kin another text. This time he knows that he needs to use a different font size. Knowing him he *will* complete the project.

171. Better to reign in hell then serve in heaven [weigh / in / nerve / then / bet / to / win / even / heat / sell]

He had the guts to challenge to measure up. Then bet that he could win by selling even that which is considered hot merchandise.

172. Why should Christians suffer? [his / double / shy / her / furs / could / faint / you]

The quality of his shy woman's furs could make you faint.

173. Wish I could help you [why / should / I / clue / p[people] / I / o[own]]

Why should I give people who I already control clues to their eventual freedom and independence?

174. Boys Choir of Harlem [yes / how / foil / harm / b[be] / o[own] / c[see]]

Yes, the best way to prevent others from harming you is to be able to foresee events for yourself.

175. Africa's deadly dozen [find / scar / a[all] / dose / delay]
[find / scared / a[all] / lay / dose]

1. The major scar is that the medicines bound for the African continent are always delayed.

2. The people also often refuse to take the medicines and devalue them because so many of the people already suffer from their bad side-effects.

176. Dmitri Kasterine [d[dumb] / e[he] / wink / I / master / it]

Dumb people still continue to use winks to throw signs to others, but I on the other hand simply master the secret modes of communication.

177. You gets no love [soft / guy / tone / e[he] / l[tell] / o[own]]
[golf / set / you? / No!] [love / no / set / " g " / you]
[no / you / set / glove(white glove)]

1. The soft guy tone is just an effort to maintain that as an image, is what he tells those closest to him.

2. Has golf paid you enough yet? No!

3. Be dependent on no click or gang. Get yourself together on your own individual merits.

4. If you refuse to cooperate you will initiate consequences… we will be forced to hit someone whom we consider to be one of our own.

178. Rep. Porter Goss [report / we / p[people] / go / ss[yes is]]
[yes / is / we / go / report / people]
[yes / is / we / people / go / report]
[yes / we / is / go / report / people]

1. We will go and report that you said: Yes.

2. If you say yes we will go and file our report.

3. Yes means we are a team. So it is a go is what we will report.

4. Yes, we agree to report people.

179. Male chauvinist pig [a[all] / c[see] / u[you] / lip / hag / feminist]

We all view you as a big-mouthed hag feminist!

180. Rep. Shelley Moore [more / he / eyes / r[ours] / pool / l[yell] / cap / it]
[more / pit / eyes / r[our] / pool / l[tell] / a[all] / c[see]]

1. The more he eyes our women the more we should yell quit it.

2. The more he eyes our women we can tell that others will eventually pick up on that fact.

181. Taliban [t[time] / I / l[yell] / ban / a[all]]
[I / ban / a[all] / l[tell] / t[time]]
[I / tell / time / all / ban]

1. It is about time that I yell ban everything.

2. I ban all watches.

3. I decide the exact time that things are to be banned.

182. Fawzi Shobokshi [if / sis / saw / book / hh[he is]]

If women have already read his book and nothing was done about it, he is who he says he is.

183. Sen. Max Baucus [men / b[be] / a[all] / u[you] / ax / cuss]
[cuss / men / be / a[all] / u[you] / ax]

1. If men are the only ones you get rid of all I can say is damn.

2. We get rid of men who cuss a lot.

184. Slowly [owl / sly]

It implies someone being and acting as sly and stealthy as an owl.

185. What it is [shit / wait]
[wit / is / hat]
[it / was / hit]

1. Do not wait.

2. Wit is intelligence

3. The expression " it " was used as a synonym for " hit " .

186. Up to isomorphism (An expression used in pure mathematics)
[u[you] / miss / him / too / pro / " p "]
[must / sip / ho(whore) / Im[I am] / poor]
[top / soup / is / how / Im[I am] / m[him]]
[most / poor / him / is / up]
[show / us / I / too / am / pimp]
[up / to / eye / sore / h[him] / peep / more]
[I / too / am / wimp / so / push / is / h[how]]

1. You apparently miss that type of professional woman also.

2. If I must engage in cunnilingus I am poor.

3. I identify with him because I too am one of the best.

4. Most poor women are exploited sexually.

5. Show everyone that I too am a pimp.

6. Until he becomes and eye sore to us he will continue to be allowed to learn from us.

7. I too must be encouraged and assisted in pursuing difficult subjects.

187. The Art of War [a[all] / r[ours] / thwart / foe]

Each branch of our armed forces is prepared to thwart a foe.

188. R.E.O. Speedwagon [Negro / saw / e[he] / dope]

The Negro *has* seen and understands the he-art!

189. Zeitgeist [get / it / is / ez(easy)]

Understanding it is an easy task.

190. Where the party at? [here / we / that / party]
[ee[he is] / threat / why / trap]
[he / wet / " y " / we / path / art] ⁵
[path / art / we / " y " / he / wet]

1. Here *we* (women) are the party.

2. He is a threat to us is why we have set the trap for him.

3. Women say he is *wet* (engages in cunnilingus), so we record all of his movements.

4. We follow his movements because we are the women he wets, and we are the women responsible for his willingness and desire to be wet.

191. Sciences [cc[see is] / I / sense]

Seeing means that one has sense ability.

192. Alexei Arbatov [I / abate / or / a[all] / flex]

Either I back off from pushing the issue or all the others will begin flexing their power also.

193. Howard Anton [o[own/] / no / hard / want]

One should be sure to always guard themselves against ever developing a monomaniac attachment to any desired object…(because it is the stuff of madness).

194. Differences [fences / if / we / dumb]

Social and emotional fences are built up by others against people seriously considered to be dumb.

195. Capital punishment [pun / meant / l[tell] / I / cap / shit]

It is a clever way of saying that I want you to tell the people that I (the State) kill people who I consider to be worthless.

196. Take you out [a[all] / key / out out [is out]]

We will not permit the *master* of the keys to be shown.

197. Gideon Yago [day / gig / o[own] / one]

Get a day job!

198. Abuzed Omar Dorda (Libyan Ambassador)
[drama / abused / door]

A negative behavior has caused an opportunity to be thwarted.

199. Nasser Al-Kidwa (Palestinian Ambassador)
[Klan /side / saw / a[all] / r[ours]]

The wrong group of people got an opportunity to gain complete insight into our private affairs.

200. Globalization [son / gloat / alibi]

When my son gloats he is hiding something from me.

201. Antonio Negri [I / aint / no / Negro]

I am not a Negro.

202. Revolution [fool / e[he] / in / rut]

He made some mistakes and now as a consequence he is experiencing an emotional low.

203. Knock yourself out [u[you] / soft / our / key / in / lock]
[OK / NY(New York City) / u[you] / felt / our / sock]
[so / loot / run / fuck / key]
[loot / fuck / run / key… / so]
[key / run / so / fuck / loot]

1. You are too soft so our master key is locked away from any current use.

2. OK New York City you have felt our figurative punch.

3. So money controls the keys to entry into the sex industry.

4. It is a monetary and a sex run key…So what!

5. The controls are in place so that illicit sex is always profitable.

204. Worst case scenario [I / can(stop) / care / so / s[street] / worst]

I quit my job so my financial situation has gotten worst.

205. Universal [I / rule / fans]

I rule over fans.

206. Universality [It / y[why] / I / rule / fans]

Full knowledge of who I really am—as celebrity—is why and how I rule over my fans.

207. Delinquency in a birth cohort [e[he] / nab / Quincy / wit / I / lend / how / hot / c[see]]

He captured me—as the vector in a game of path art (music)—and now I am explaining how the wit of the lexicon works.

208. Nobody has our sources [sour / course / had / no / boys]
[boys / had / no / sour / source]
[hours / around / boss / yo(flow) / e[he] / c[see]]
[sour / boys / had / no / source]

1. The boring course had little support.

2. The boys themselves had fascinating tutelage.

3. One who spends a lot of time around the job's boss will get the best chance to see how the everyday operations really work.

4. Angry men have typically had dysfunctional upbringings.

I Am A Key

209. Theorem [we / o[own] or [owe] / them]
(mathematics uses the *inclusive* " or ".)

We *own* them (theorems) and / or we *owe* the use of them.

210. Name of the rose [those / name / e[he] / for]
[forename / those]
[name / those / e[he] / for]
[for / those / he / name]
[those / for / he / name]

1. He approves of those names.

2. Design or create names for them.

3. Name the persons that he has approved.

4. We support those whom he has given names to.

5. Name the ones that have been found to truly believe in him.

211. Foucault's Pendulum [soul / cult / map / fend / uu [you is]]
[soul / cult / map / you / is / fend]
[soul / cult / map / you / is / " f " / end]

1. You are a fend (fence) for the Black cults that control path art.

2. You are an unwitting fend because you are one of those being mapped.

3. If the cult maps you one of your ends in society is to receive the " f " rating.

212. Definitions [I / sit / find / on / e[me]] [sit / I / find / one]
[i.e. / sit / on / find]

1. I am the one who sits and writes about what intellectually is to be found on me.

2. *If I sit as myself I wish to be found out.*

3. That is, I need to oversee what I find out.

213. Notion [I / no / into] [no / I / not]

1. I am not into it.

2. No, I am not.

214. Abstract [cab / stat / r[ours]]
[bac[k] / sta[b] / r[ours]]
[star / b[be] / act]

1. Those taxicab statistics are ours.

2. Backstab our own.

3. Someone is pretending to be a star (celebrity).

215. Tax-deferred annuity [try / wax / fee / a[all] / dd [is done] / n[in]]
[nite [night] / try / wax / fan / ee [he is] / dud]
[try / fee / wax / dd [dumb is] / a[all] / n[in]]
[" y " / refer / dude / at[after] / nn[is in] / taxi]
[any / tit / n[in] / ax / refer / dude]

1. Try to put a contract out on someone and you will get caught.

2. Someone failed to successfully execute a night time hit.

3. Trying to pay for a contract on someone means all that are involved are dumb.

4. A woman gets into a taxicab and refers to the driver as dude.

5. Get rid of any woman in our organization who refers to a man as dude.

6. Every woman in our organization must stop referring to men as dude.

216. Exponential Functions [exact / point / one / l[yell] / sin / fun]

The point is that some people refer to *sin* as fun.

217. **Elliptical Functions** [lip / fun / tells / action / I / c[see]]

   1. Talking about having fun explains the kind of activities I generally am involved in or the kind of activities that I monitor.

   2. Public speaking is the kind of thing I enjoy doing.

218. **Robert Tools** (artificial heart recipient)
   [wow / tools / be / t[time]]

   The exclamation of " wow " as an expression of astonishment over how mechanical devices (tools) can extend life.

219. **Alan Dershowitz** [how / we / lands / a[all?] / sit]
   [s[yes] / we / sit / a[all] / land / how]
   [ho(whore) / slander / wits / a[all]]

   1. We just sit at our desks, do what we do best, and the offers come our way.

   2. Yes we sit and study is how we all learn.

   3. Slandering whores is the wellspring of our wit.

220. **Try again** [r[ours] / aint / gay]

   Our people are not gay!

221. **Fermat's Last Theorem** [fast / master / we / o[owe] / them / l[tell]]
   [fast / master / we / l[yell] / o[own] (adopt, sponsor, support, and/or identify with) / them]

   1. We owe conceptual assistance to those graduate students who are fast learners of the subject of mathematics.

   2. We adopt and support graduate mathematics students who are fast learners.

222. **"Fossett Aborts Balloon Mission, Lands in Brazil"** [born / brazen / I / floss / ballasts / I / miss / land / I / toot / on]

Born arrogant, I promote and secure sponsors for my global balloon flights. If I have to abort a flight and miss land there are provisions already made for my rescue.

223. "Balloon trip aborted" [trap / tool / we / bail / bond]

The tool we use to trap the accused into appearing as promised in court is the bail bond.

224. Algebra [grab / ale]
[rage / lab]
[leg / a / bra]
[real / gab]
[wage / lab]
[we / b[be] / a / gal]

1. Grab a beer.

2. This is a rage laboratory…where we study anger and ways to manage anger.

3. The expression "leg" is synonymous with the expression "bra", and both simply mean a female.

4. Someone who is verbose has the gift of gab.

5. This is a wage laboratory…where we make money studying ways to make money.

6. The term " we " in this context is synonymous with the expression "gal" , and they both simply mean a female.

225. Abstract Algebra [lab / wage / tab / st[street] / car]
[t[time] / race / tabs / lab / rage]
[real / brat / gab / l[tell] / st[street] / c[see]]
[slab / act / tab / r[our] / rage]

1. Make money and buy a car.

2. It is time for the Black race to be more constantly and keenly vigilant over societal actions towards them, and *yet* learn

individually to master how best to keep their ***environmentally induced rage*** in check…that is, under control.

3. The real trouble makers are those big mouths who explain how the streets are able to see things.

4. A homicide or suicide is induced when one is simply unable to *not tabulate* or forget bad experiences and thoughts resulting in their intensifying their own level of frustration and rage over time.

226. Robert Hormats [how / tame / st[street] / rob / r[ours]]
   [tame / how / t[time] / robs / r[ours]]
   [t[time] / tame / how / robs / r[ours]]
   [t[time] / robs / how / r[hours] / tame]

1. The method is to tame or humble us by breaking our spirit, so that the street is easily able to rob us of our natural inheritance as people.

2. *By developing a subdued or cultivated spirit one only believes in* **the prescribed** *ways of doing things, so that wasted time in that effort in effect robs us of life's bounties…those that are secured through* ***free enterprise activities and outlook***.

3. *Once tamed those who know simply exploit us…as consumers.*

4. Time robs us by dulling our spirits when we are encouraged to be obliged to spend hours and hours of unnecessary time to accomplish uncertain goals.

5. With the major portion of our lifetime already wasted utilizing new insight on how to quickly accomplish things and be successful is tamed by there being so little time remaining in life to accomplish them.

227. Moody Blues [me / sold / o[own] / buy]
   [dye / mob / soul]
   [some / b[be] / y[why] / loud]

1. Since I have sold myself—my own spirit—to the devil I am relegated to being a consumer only.

2. Exchange roles and circumstances and Blacks would run society in the same way.

3. Some succeed in becoming extremely successful. Why? Because they remained loud or uncultivated. That is, they simply remained true to their own natural inner spirit.

228. Clive Cussler [if / cuss / e[he] / c[see] / well]

If cursed he sees what is going on in society too well.

229. Alice Kaplan [I / lack / a[all] / e[me] / plan]

I lack an **all me**—*my personal interest only*—**plan**.

230. The Collaborator [labor / e[he] / color / that]

He has attached a racial color to those who are predominantly assigned to be laborers.

231. The door is open [tire / so / pooh / end] [so / die / poor / then]
[so / poor / die / then]

1. You have become exhausted and weary from the struggle so you will have a contemptuous and resentful end.

2. So die poor then.

3. When your plight is poverty your spirit dies a slow and painful death.

232. " Along Came A Spider " [lease / can / go / m[him] /
paid / r[ours]]
[measle(s) / can / go / rapid]
[I / d[done] / rap / can / go / l[tell] / m[him] / easy]
[l[tell] / m[him] / d[dumb] / can / go / I / rap / easy]

1. He can violate his lease because he has satisfied our requirements.

2. The measles can spread rapidly.

3. Tell him that I (Easy) said that when I am done rap music can go.

4. *When criminal convictions have routinely been diminished we can tell that opportunities in society have been opened through improved individual participation in society and in their understanding of how the system works.*

5. Tell him that being dumb can go, I rap easily.

233. Aces and Eights [yes / ace / is / nigh / date]

Yes, our ace is closely approaching his/her appointed time.

234. Megan Rose [same / Negro]

He/she is that same Negro.

235. Never be the same again [saw / a or a[all] / gain / then / fee / me / be]

Once all others can see a gain I will profit from it!

236. Alex Cross [saw / lex[lexicon] / c[see] / so!]
[saw / lexicon / so / see]
[s[yes] / o[own] / see/ saw / lexicon]
[see / saw / lexicon / so!]

1. Power the secret of the lexicon has been seen! So what!

2. You have seen the secret of the lexicon so begin to see—understand—more clearly.

3. Yes, our own chosen has seen the secret of the lexicon.

237. Rob Sobhani [be / o[own] / is / how / a[all] / sin]

It is paradoxical that according to the principle of State control being your own person is how all people come to be labeled as having **sinned**…become deviant.

238. Tiger Woods [wires / to / God]

He appears to have direct communications with God.

239. Barry Bonds [barn / dry / so / b[be]]

He is basically naïve and innocent so leave him be.

240. Tommy Hilfiger [my / gift / home / I / l[tell] / r[ours]]
[home / my / gift / I / l[yell] / r[hours]]

1. I told my friends that I gave away a home as a gift.
2. I received a home as a gift and I yelled happily for hours.

241. Old Navy [d[dumb] or [dark(Blacks) / l[yell] / ofay / n[in]]
[Old / Fay / n[in]]

1. Dumb people yell there is an ofay—white person—involved with us.
2. Blacks yell whites into this level of understanding.
3. An old white person is involved in our business.

242. You know [y[why] / o[owe] / u[you] / k[ok] / now]

Why put yourself in debt when you can now afford to pay for everything up front?!

243. Cause I aint got no money [c[see] / gain / use / meant / o[owe] / yin / too]

To understand and gain use of something not owned by you means that you owe money then too.

244. Motherfucker [fume / other / c[see] / r[ours] / k[ok]]

1. Make the others angry but see that our people are ok.
2. *Use menus that make the other people fart and make sure our people are all ok.*

245. Our assurance of safety in uncertain times [you / o[owe] / me / sin / ass / is / certain / you / after / fan / cunt]

Inviting a female fan into your celebrity private quarters or dressing room is called a "you owe me sin". That action almost insures that the fan would feel indebted to you, so having a contrived type of consensual sex with the fan would almost be a certainty. Conclusion: you invited the fan in because you were after her cunt.

246. Emotions and relationships [hips / motions / a[c]tions / we(female) / land / e[he]]

Men can be easily aroused and wooed by the way in which a woman is physically shaped and motions her hips and body.

247. God can hear the blood [hood / bear / gloat / he / c[see] / n[in]]

When a racist cop gloats he seizes or has seized the opportunity to pounce on a person of color.

248. The sound of innocent blood [o[owe] / inn / cent / so / th[that] / blood / e[he] / found]

1. He was located because he paid for his hotel room with a credit card.
2. Investigators tracked down a Black man because it appears he owed an Inn keeper some money.

249. Hick [h[he] / I / c[see] / k[ok]]

If I comprehend the methods of the he-art then I am considered to be able to see ok.

250. Ayaz Amir (I as a mirror—phonetic) [say / all / I / am / is / ours] ours / is / all / I / am / say]

I am only the product of my biography and social environment.

251. Al-Qaeda [leada[leader] / q[cue] / a[all]] [cue / all / is / deal]

1. The leader is to give instructions to all.

2. The deal is that everyone is to receive instructions.

252. Barnett Rubin [bar / bet / nut[cum] / win]

A group of men at a bar wager on whether or not a particular member of their group has the savoir faire to woo and have sexual intercourse with a selected female patron. The assigned member who accepts the wager wins the bet if he is successful.

253. Receiving [we / c[see] / g[game] / I / fine]

1. If the woman appreciates game then I am fine.

2. We see the object and she is *fine*...a pretty woman!

254. There's no finish [wish / those / n[in] / fine]

1. Wish everyone we are involved with well.

2. Wish everyone you know succcss in finding a beautiful mate.

255. Hodja Bahaudeen [do / a[all] / u[you] / had / been / Haj]

Destroy all of you had been our battle cry.

256. Rush out and get some [use / grant / o[owe] / shout / me / d[dumb]]
[o[own] / me / d[dumb] / grant / use / shout]

Anyone who permits them self to be exploited is dumb.

257. Muhammad Atef [a[all] / math / fame / mud or dum[b]]

People actually have little respect for mathematics or mathematicians.

258. I think [h[he] / ink / it]
[ink / it / h[he]]

He put it in writing and got in trouble.

259. Fuck [" f " / u[you] / c[see] / k[ok]]
[f[fuck] / u[you] / k[ok] / c[see]]

1. An " f " rating means that you comprehend *he-art*, and it also necessarily means that you are aware of the existence of *path art*.

2. I can say fuck you to those of you who comprehend the (above… my emphasis) *arts*.

260. Twenty biblical principles for debt release [Bible / people / wince / went / be / as / if / s[yes] / ditty / call / is / ours]
[Bible / people / wince / if / call / went / be / witty / as / r[ours?] / d[dumb] / s[yes!]]

Black church goers have historically expressed a great deal of dismay over and an unwillingness to any longer associate themselves with gospel singers who have converted to what is referred to as *secular music*…for monetary gain.

261. It's about going out with the band and doing your own thing
[ban / doing / your / out / thing / go / with / it / then / guts / in / b[be] / a[all] / o[own]]
[ban / doing / your / out / thing / go / with / it / then / su[e] / boating / dad]
[ban / doing / your / out / thing / go / with / it / then / dad / guts / in / b[be] / a[all] / o[own]]

1. Do not be so quick to quit a depressing job where your co-workers actions often discourage you. It is not infrequent that negative co-worker attitudes change somewhat when they see that one has the wherewithal to persevere.

2. Do not be so quick to resign from a depressing job. Allow your solace and redemption to be the stability, freedom, and independence you get from your maintaining a continuous or stable income over time.

3. Avoid being so quick to quit a depressing job. Your perseverance will win you a lot of familial support, pride, and respect.

262. Homeland Security Swearing In [in / swear / to / secure / land / him / yin / g[game]]

Our leaders will be granted whatever funding they need if they swear to secure and defend our land.

263. On my way [no / way / m[him] / " y " or why]
[" y " / is / woman]

1. There is no way that *he* (as in the subject in the he-art) can be female.

2. In no way is he responsible.

3. The symbol " y " refers to a woman or female.

264. The Worst Birthday [story / be / width / thaw]

When the story is allowed to be told it means there is a thaw in our frigid control over a wide range of knowledge.

265. Dobby's Warning [sing(music) / yarn / bow / b[be] / d[dumb]]

To inform people of how and why music is more than just a romantic story-line in a melody is a stupid act.

266. The Burrow [bt[bet] or [beat] / hue / r[ours] / wow]
[hue / bt[beat] or [bet] / r[ours] / wow]

1. When whites defeat Blacks in anything competitive they get very excited.

2. Whites are astonished when Blacks defeat them in anything competitive.

267. At Flourish and Blotts [that / s[o]ot / is / flour / bland]
[flo[flow] / at[after] / u[you] / wish / a[all] / nd[need] / Blot / ts[test] (Rorschach Test)]
[at[after] / flo[flow] / u[you] / wish / a[all] / nd[need] / blot / ts[test] (*psychological testing*)]
[float / u[you] / wish / a[all] / nd[need] / blot / ts[test]]

1. *Many white people are of the opinion that Blacks do not have as much range of character and emotional substance as do whites.*

2. *Many whites wish it or understand that Black people's efforts to emulate the best that they see in them, and compete with whites in essential ways is so stressful that it results in Blacks frequently having emotional breakdowns.*

3. *Most whites are very secure and confident in—even gloat over—the historical social advantage that they have over Blacks. Many whites want Blacks to know that they wish that Blacks will be driven crazy in their effort to compete with them for the purpose of establishing a more level playing field.*

268. The Whomping Willow [who / willing / pow / them]

Whoever is willing shoot them or blow them up!… (them?)

269. Gilderoy Lockhart [gild (guild)/ we / yo[flow] / lock / h[e]art]
[gild / we / lock / h[e]art / yo[flow]]

In considering ourselves (whites or women) a **guild** we wish to put a lock on one's ability to learn about the he- art.

270. Mud Bloods and Murmurs [sum / land / woods / rum / dumb]

Many Black people believe that most white people are *rum dumb*. That is, they believe whites are a *queer or peculiar* people who **actually are** insensitive to the real plight of Black people.

271. The Death Day Party [hey / dear / day / tt[time is] / path]
[death / day / they / part]

1. Hey dear, the path to success is through securing a day job and that type of work is intimidating to many.

2. Keep a good job until it is time to retire or you expire.

272. The Writing On The Wall [th[r]ew / wit / in / th[that] / wall / gone]
[tie / in / th[that] / the / wrong / wall]
[wall / tie / in / th[that] / the / wrong]

1. Knowledge of how wit works has entered into the writing game so that wall is gone.

2. Any effort to use the church for blinders is the wrong wall.

3. Any effort to wall in the church is the ultimate wrong.

273. The Rogue Bludger [there / u[you] / go / lug / be / r[are] or [our] / d[dumb]]
[rude / go / there / b[be] / lug]

1. There you have it a lug is a stupid person.

2. Rude people say it aloud: that person is stupid.

274. The Dueling Club [thing / due / b[be] / l[tell] / clue]

What is overdue is to be given a clue.

275. The Polyjuice Potion [tie / o[own] / joy / punch / top / lie]

If church leaders believe that they have ownership and possession of everything that can elicit true joy, then that church sentiment is a major lie.

276. The Very Secret Diary [the / cry / fey / see / wart / I.D.]

The person fated to die soon has been identified as an objectionable person.

277. Cornelius Fudge [I[eye] / clone / d[dumb] / rug / fuse]
[I[eye] / fuse / clone / d[dumb] / rug]

1. Those persons whom " *Eye* " (review anagram # 135) has created and labeled dumb can be identified because Eye has mysteriously attached a rectal condyloma on them.[6]

2. Eye has caused one of its clones to become enraged—and driven to madness—because it has attached one of its mysterious *rugs* (rectal condyloma) on them.

278. Aragog [aa[all is] / r[ours] / o[own] / gg[is game]]

All of the best that wisdom has to offer belongs to wisdom. The only thing that the rest of us as everyday people can own is how best—as individuals—to play wisdom's games.

279. The Chamber of Secrets [Crete / thef[t] / bar / me / c[see] / h[he] / o[own] / ss[secrets] or [secret service]]
[Crete / thef[t] / bar / c[see] / ho / mess]

1. The Greek authorities stole wisdom's secrets and barred others from seeing the sources of the theft and how they themselves have kept the best of the information secret.

2. The perpetrators of the Greek theft barred everyday people from understanding that the wit of the he-art is based on the slandering and the pandering of whores.

280. The Heir of Slythewin [the / sly / win / fe[e] / their / ho]
[their / flo[flow] / y[why] / he / win / the / s[yes]]
[their / o[own] / fly / he / win / the / s[yes]]
[he / o[own] / fly / s[yes] / their / the / win]

1. Successful men often have a secret mistress.

2. Women are easily attracted to wealthy men.

3. If a man can help support an unmarried woman and her kids, he can readily win an intimate sexual liaison or relationship with her.

4. If a man is wealthy enough to own his own airplane, he can win over most women that he might be interested in.

281. Dobby's Reward [boys / r[ours] / be / dd[dumb is] / war]
[boys / r[hours] / be / dd[done is] / war]

To call our boys dumb and act to curtail their freedoms and pleasures is an act of war.

282. J. K. Rowling [owl / King / c[see] / r[ours]]
[c[see] / wink / low / g[game]]

1. A vigilant King (leader) understands the street.

2. Understand that frequent winking to indicate a sign implies one's limited knowledge of the street game.

283. Harry Potter [why / pot? / we / art!]
[why / we / to / part]

1. The question is why do we smoke pot? We smoke pot because we are artists and smoking pot enhances our creative senses.

2. Why we are to be separate!?

284. The Protestant Ethic and the Spirit of Capitalism
[t[time] / he / protest / ant / ethic / n[in] / d[done] / t[time] / he / wit / o[only] / f[first] / capital / is / m[made]]
[he / protest / ant / ethic / n[in] / d[done] / tt[is time] / he / wit / own / if / man / list(key) / capa[ble]]

1. By the time our student understands enough to firmly and confidently begin protesting the ***workaholic*** ethic his training is complete. Moreover, his command of wit is only then sufficiently mature for him to begin making money.

2. When he is informed enough and prepared to protest the ***workaholic*** ethic our protégé has completed our course of study. This ***man*** can now teach his own students, ***if he has mastered the use of a key***.

285. Nuclear Energy [n[in] (inside) / u[you] / clear / e[he] / new / gy[guy] (or woman)]

When you are clear and certain in the knowledge of who you are inside of you as an individual you are a new person.

286. Understanding Elementary Algebra with Geometry: A Course for College Students
[understand / my / gallery / brats / colleagues / he / wanting / wit / force / or / tee(peg) / men / e[we] / geo(the earth) / stud]

[understand / my / gallery / brats / colleagues / wit / force

/ wanting / he / or / tee(peg) / men / e[we] / geo(the earth) / stud]

1. Understand that as new graduates you are yet my little immature spectators and that my colleagues are seeking a league of men who are willing to promote our schooling and educate other people in this knowledge. Otherwise men each of you will be considered nothing more than a stud to us.

2. Understand new graduates that my colleagues want to recruit you to join our wit force. Otherwise they will simply label you international studs.

287. Lord of the Rings: The Two Towers [how / world / sting / h[her] / foe / to / sweet / r[our] / t[time]]
[world / hint / goes / f[fuck] / the / two / towers]

1. It (9/11) is how the nether world collectively stung her (U.S.A.), and our eternal foes thought they would sweeten or improve their own status on the earth in our time.

2. How did our foe manage to accomplish it world? We allowed a sting from our foe, and that was done to increase and protect our longevity as a civilized nation and member of civil society.

3. Our hint to the world goes: Fuck the two towers!

288. Frank Sinatra [" F " / ranks / in / r[ours] / at[after] / a[all]]

You see an " f " rating ***does*** rank in our scheme of things after all!

Endnotes

(*) An asterisk (anagrams # 3 and # 70) means that I have added and inserted an additional anagram or another item in a proximate location to aid in the clarity of the discussion.

1. The expression " he-art "—as discussed in chapter one of **The Mind Factory**—refers to the *subtle* and historically secret art of training individuals—both male and female— in the mastery of the most sophisticated forms of streetwise adult knowledge and information gathering.

2. The word " car " in this context is another expression for the word " hit ".

3. The expression " Joe " means " the government " here.

4. The expression " wet " here means to make a person bloody by *shooting* them.

5. The expression " path art " refers to the existence of a scientific technique and process whereby a selected individual's discrete lifelong activities are monitored, keyed, and recorded for purposes related to the *keying* of the written word. While I know that this practice exists, I do not understand enough of the critical details of how it works to discuss it formally. Moreover, since it represents an even more profound secret than what is being discussed here, I am not entirely sure it is something that can be discussed formally and publically.

6. Apparently, some people fear the ostensible consequences of having this surgically removed; so they retain and attempt to conceal this growth on their bodies.

Summary

For the benefit of those who do not understand that they do themselves a disservice by reading the last chapter in a book *before* they read the first, I will avoid writing anything that might shock your sensibilities, confuse you, or disappoint your expectations as could happen when one reads the last chapter of **The Mind Factory**... in the above order. In the present brief summary chapter I will only relate a few *simple* truths.

The interpretations that I am presenting in this book are *absolutely not* provided for the sake of the reader agreeing with their content. As a matter of fact, *the writer* has no way of knowing in advance exactly what the content of the derivations of an anagram will reveal. A meaningful content can only completely surface once the derivation and its interpretation is completed. Moreover, once an anagram is completed, the anagram will possess its own truth and that truth whether or not one agrees with it. What matters is that one acknowledge the reality of the latent content of an expression, and develops an appreciation for the *experience* of having new, unexpected information revealed to themselves through their work in deriving anagrams. Additionally it is essential the reader appreciates that the content and meaning of an anagram—derived from a given expression—will immediately vary based on its writer's personal knowledge. The personal knowledge which creates *unique* mental images informed by the writer's individual experiences, how worldly-wise the writer is, the writer's world view, and his/her *outlook*...that is, point of view.

This is a subjective enterprise and the *participant observer* slash *researcher* will continue indefinitely to be involved in a very steep learning curb. Learning things that one never knew or expected to know is what this enterprise is all about. Some of what one discovers will underscore and crystallize their common sense understanding. Other discoveries will expand their range of vision, heighten their sensibilities, and create new mental images of reality within them. Most poignantly and pointedly it will affirm and advance what *is* reality.

Of course one could argue and be justified in arguing that this theory of anagrams and consequent information gathering is some pretty abstract stuff. Yet, there is one thing among other things with respect to my exposition and application of this theory that lets me know the theory is grounded and therefore my intellectual feet are firmly on the ground. It is such an obvious thing that it may well have gone unnoticed—overlooked or taken for granted—by many readers while reviewing the above anagrams. It is not simply that the content of the anagrams have meaning in each of our everyday lives, because they certainly do. What is *unique* and gives perfect *verification* and *reliability* to the theory is that when one examines the content of the *derivation and interpretation* for many of the anagrams developed from a person's name—especially given this relatively small group of randomly selected anagrams—, *the meanings found in the names* of those *real* individuals in real time in our everyday world speaks directly to what those name sake individuals actually do or have done in real time in our everyday world. Whether the reader initially recognizes it or not, this immediate observation is a demonstration of or is proof of the truth of the theory. That is, the theory that argues that information about what we do and have done in our everyday world is embedded as latent content in our language. It also hints at why and how it may well be possible to predict future behavior by way of the interpretation of the written word…as theorists have suggested it is.

Many people are afraid to take these formal excursions and venture into the realms of understanding being discussed and examined in my books. In most other instances, people are simply not interested in reading anything resembling formal modes of thought, so even the few *fun* pages of this current book would bore them. If so, so be it! They *only* fail to understand the relationship of common sense to formal thought and that of formal thought to common sense. In truth neither one is any less difficult to master than the other and, in my opinion, they both possess similar powers of observation and are developed for the very same purposes… understanding and then managing the affairs of our everyday world. The information issuing from anagrams leads most directly to the mastery of common sense, by opening a window to a panorama of atypical yet useful information on that level. So if the reader will have the courage and I have piqued their curiosity enough, the key that I have supplied provides the means by which virtually anyone can pursue this rarefied intellectual journey.

References

Johnson, Larry Odell. <u>The Mind Factory: the ability to cipher information is a secret of the lexicon.</u> Indiana: 1st Books Library, 2002, 2003.

About The Author:

Larry Odell Johnson is an Assistant Professor of Mathematics, Emeritus. In 2004, he took early retirement after thirteen plus years of teaching at Dutchess Community College in Upstate New York. A former police officer and Federal Bureau of Prisons Intern, Larry is a graduate of Arizona State University and the University of California at Berkeley. Larry has degrees in Mathematics and Criminology. In addition, he is two courses shy of a Master's in Mathematics from the State University of New York at Albany and has completed all of the course work towards a Doctorate in Criminology at U. C. Berkeley. Larry says that issues related to having to work, situational politics, and waning interests have prevented him from completing these two additional advanced degrees. This is his second book, and he has previously published several articles in the now defunct academic journal **Issues In Criminology.** Although Larry has skills in higher mathematics, one of his favorite pastimes is doing research in social science. His interest in ***anagrams*** was ignited during the mid 1970's, while he was doing research in the subject area of the Sociology of Knowledge and in the throes of completing his course work towards the doctorate degree.

www.ingramcontent.com/pod-product-compliance
Ingram Content Group UK Ltd.
Pitfield, Milton Keynes, MK11 3LW, UK
UKHW041955230426
12048UKWH00008B/359